Notes By Al

Notes By Al

My musical knowledge of notes was very limited. I didn't know notes and couldn't read them.

These songs are all by ear. I would write the lyrics as they came to me, put my tune to the lyrics, sing it to a cassette tape, give it to a friend of mine who would then arrange it to lead sheet or song.

Just thought these might be interesting. Some even got published.

bye

Al Vicent

Order this book online at www.trafford.com
or email orders@trafford.com

Most Trafford titles are also available at major online book retailers.

Print information available on the last page.

ISBN: 978-1-6987-1451-6 (sc)
ISBN: 978-1-6987-1450-9 (e)

Trafford rev. 04/19/2023

Trafford
PUBLISHING® www.trafford.com

North America & international
toll-free: 844-688-6899 (USA & Canada)
fax: 812 355 4082

TABLE OF CONTENTS

GONNA SEE A BABY

BEACON CHORAL SERIES

Gonna See A Baby was originally published by Beacon Hill Music in 1980. It was a part of the Beacon Choral Series. The musical score was composed by Robert Brown. It was written for a flute accompaniment to be played with a joyful manner.

GONNA SEE A BABY

(S.A.T.B. with Optional Flute)

ROBERT BROWN   **AL VICENT**

*Start here in absence of flute.

Where's ev-'ry-bod-y go - in', please tell me.

Gon-na see a ba-by in a Beth-a-le - hem.

Why's ev-'ry-bod - y rush - in', please tell me.

There's been a ba - by born in

We've been a look-in' for a   Mar - y and Jo - seph.

Beth-a - le - hem.   Gon-na see a

Heard from an an - gel 'bout _____ a lit-tle ba - by.

ba-by born in Beth-a - le - hem.

Born in a man-ger in a Beth-a - le - hem.

1. Born in the Spir - it, born in glo -
2. Come to___ help the wea - ry soul,

- ry.

Come from the Fa - ther,
Heal the ___ wound and

tell the sto - ry.
make us whole. _____

Look-in' o - ver

Shin-in' on a sta-ble in a   Beth-a - le - hem.

yon - der I   think I see a bright star

Why is all the shep - herds star - in' in the man - ger?

Look-in' at the ba - by born in

Beth - a - le - hem.

Why is all the peo - ple bring-in' pres-ents to the ba - by?

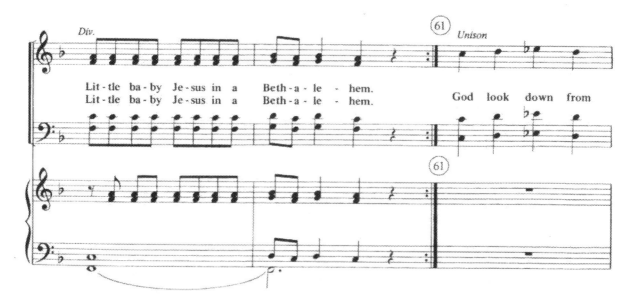

up a - bove, _____ Give to us a ba - by in a Beth - a - le - hem.

Send to us His per - fect love, _____ Send His Son Je - sus to show His

love.

SON OF THE HIGHEST

The second time Gonna See A Baby was published was by Lillenas Publishing Co. in 1983. It was A Choral Presentation for Christmas. It was arranged by Dick Bolks with Drama by Paul M. Miller. The songbook is set up like a play with different song leading you through from the beginning to the end of the Christmas story.

GONNA SEE A BABY

ROBERT BROWN
Arr. by Dick Bolks

AL VICENT

Joyful (♩=176)

Narrator: So it was to the shepherds that God first announced the birth of His Son. To

shepherds came word of One who would become the Good Shepherd and who would know
His sheep.

With excitement
Tenor solo

Where's ev - 'ry - bod - y go -

19

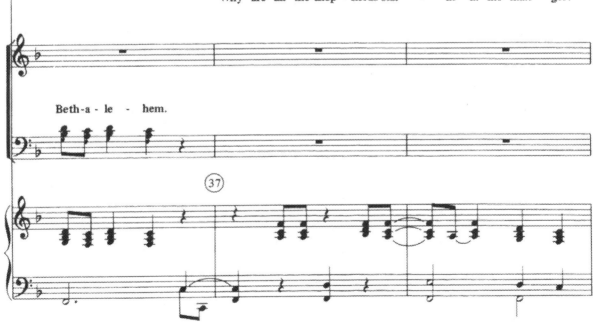

Why all the fuss-in' o - ver just a lit - tle Ba - by?

Sent from-a heav-en to

show - a God's love.

1. See that star, it shines so bright,_____
2. Come to help our pain and grief,_____

23

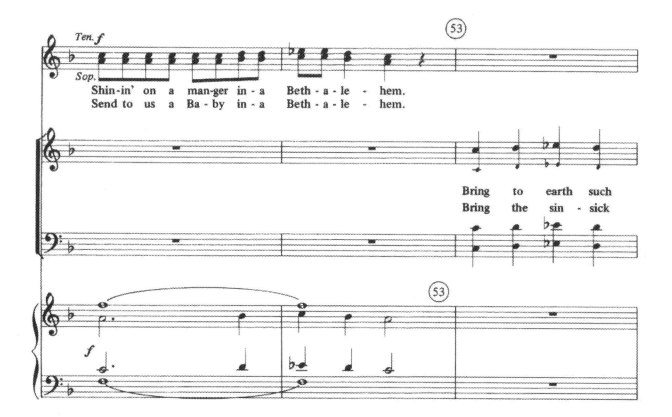

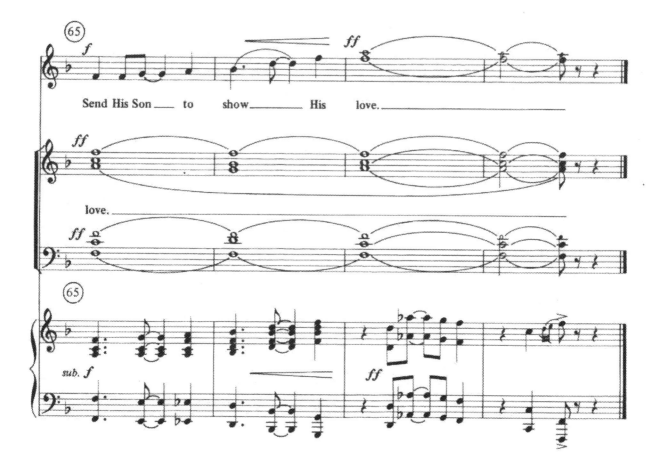

Send His Son ____ to show ____ His love. ____

love. ____

TABLEAU: SHEPHERDS make their way to stable and shyly enter. They kneel at the manger through following narration and song.

Narrator: And they came in haste and found their way to Mary and Joseph, and Baby Jesus as He lay in the manger.

Man 1: And those shepherds were so convinced that they had seen the Son of God . . .

Man 2: That they told everyone they met along the way.

Narrator: And all who heard the news wondered at the marvelous things they told them.

Woman: But Mary treasured all this, pondering it in her heart.

CHRISTMAS A CAPPELLA

The third time Gonna See A Baby was published was again by
Lillenas Publishing Co., this time in 2001. It was part of a
group of 23 Creative Arrangements for Choirs Large & Small.
It was arranged by Tom Fettke.

GONNA SEE A BABY

ROBERT BROWN
Arranged by Tom Fettke

AL VICENT

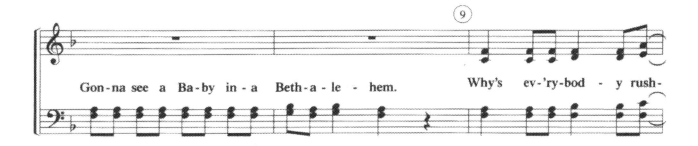

Shin - in' on a sta - ble in a Beth - a - le - hem.
Du, du, du, Du, du, du.

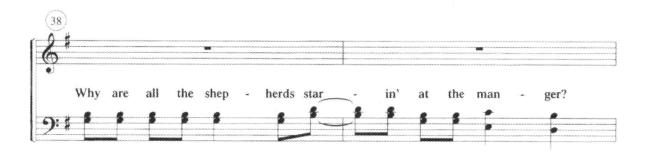

Why are all the shep - herds star - - in' at the man - ger?

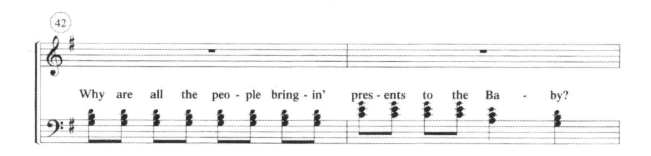

Look - in' at the Ba - by born in Beth - a - le - hem.
Du, du, du, Du, du, du.

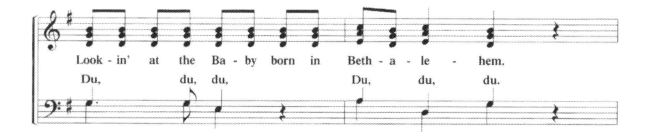

Why are all the peo - ple bring - in' pres - ents to the Ba - by?

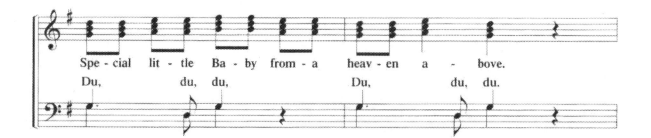

Spe - cial lit - tle Ba - by from a heav - en a - bove.
Du, du, du, Du, du, du.

God looked down from up a - bove,

Gave to us a Ba - by in a Beth - a - le - hem.

Sent to us His per - fect love,

Sent His Son, Je - sus, sent His Son, Je - sus, Sent His Son,

love.

Je - sus, to show His love, His glo - rious love.

love.

THE TRAIN OF LIFE

THE TRAIN OF LIFE

Arr. by GIANNI STAIANO

AL VICENT

train would start when one was ve-ry ve-ry small   and once it would start you were then on   call This

train was on   the road of life   and each one drove from birth all through life

As a   per-son got old ~ er then the road got rough And the

each one drove from birth all through life   there were

ma-ny temp ta - tions on the road of life   but signs were there to keep the dri-ver think-in'right This

train was   on   the road of life   and each one drove   from birth all through life

God and his an - gels were at the last stop each train tried hard to get to this stop This

train was on the road of life and each one drove from birth all through life This

train it was a run-nin in a vis-ion in the night This train it was a run-nin in a vis-ion in the night a

run-nin a run-nin a run-nin a run-nin This train was a run-nin in the night This

train was a run-nin in the night

rall. _ _ _ _ _ _ _ _ _ _ _ _ _ _ _ _

EXCUSE ME

EXCUSE ME

AL VICENT

Ex-cuse me please but did you hap-pen to see Je - sus For I was told that he might pass this way to - day That he might stop share his

bless-ings and min-gle with us   Ex-cuse me please but did you

see him_____ pass this way to- day?   oh if he

passed   did he leave   a mes-sage   Was there a

sign   that he might pass   this way a - gain   Did he

stop   heal the sick   and help the low - ly?   Ex-cuse me

please but did you see Je sus........ pass this way to- day?

None passed this way ex cept the stran-ger who said, Come let the lit-tle chil-dren sit on my knee. But they said the stran ger's arms were open wide and from somewhere deep down in - side That love just flowed and in it's

più mosso

meno mosso

way came through to you   to you to stay   to you to   stay

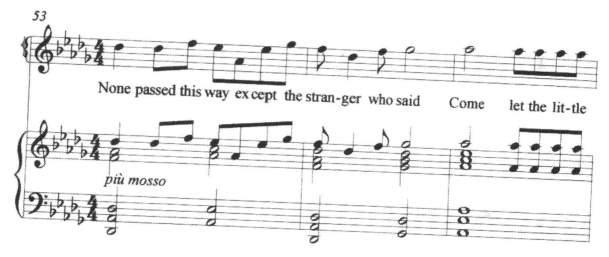

None passed this way ex cept the stran-ger who said   Come   let the lit-tle

più mosso

chil - dren sit on my   knee.   Ex-cuse me   please   may-be the

meno mosso

stran - ger   was   Je - sus   Ex-cuse me please   may-be the

stran - ger   was   Je - sus   Who passed this

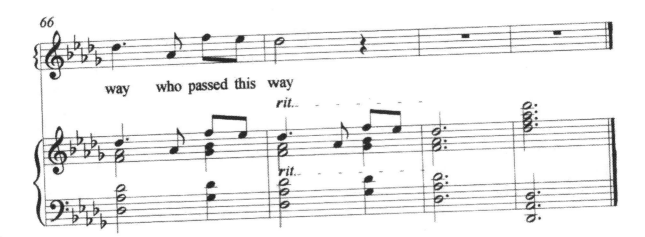

way   who passed this way

rit. - - - - - - - - - -

THE WAYS OF GOD

THE WAYS OF GOD

AL VICENT

THERE'S A REASON

THERE'S A REASON

Arr. by GIANNI STAIANO

AL VICENT

Slow Gospel swing

I. There's a

rea - son for the sun - shine in the sky There's a
rea - son that God sends his love each day To each

rea - son why the birds fly by on high For this is
one in his own ve - ry spe - cial way For this is

love in Na - ture's way for love al - ways finds a way There's a
love from God a - bove and God's love it finds a way

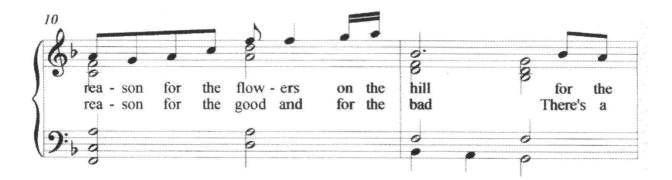

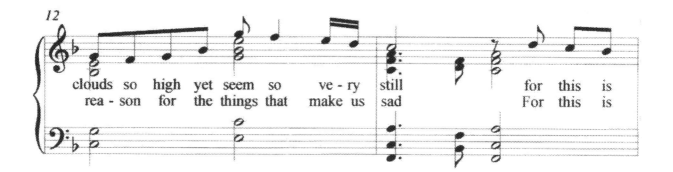

A FLAG

A FLAG

AL VICENT

SALINAS

SALINAS

Cowboy Waltz

AL VICENT

skies and green fields seem to call me___ ev - er
soft moon filled nights in the val - ley___ might make

si - lent ev - er love-ly___ in my mind Sa -
you want to___ stay in___ that___ town

li- nas___ Sa - li- nas___ Sa - li- nas___ Oh you

call out so clear - ly to me Sa -

li- nas___ Sa - li- nas___ Sa - li- nas___ A

ci - ty___ in the Gold - en val- ley___

RUTH

RUTH

AL VICENT

Gospel Swing

Ruth_ was a lad - y_ from the Mo - a - bite_ la - nd She mar - ried her hus - band on

God's com - mand They lived hap - py in the Mo - a - bite_ la - nd 'till

God called Ruth's hus band_ to his hea - ven - ly home Af - ter - Ruth's hus - band had

pas - sed a - way_ Ruth went to Beth - le - hem with Na - o - mi to stay_

She gleaned bar - ley in the field_ each day_ 'till Bo - az seen her work ing_ and took

no - tice of her_ Ruth Ruth Go - d loves you_

God's spi - rit glows in you_ Ruth Ruth

love's_ in you_ Love real - ly shines in you_

A SONG CAN GO ANYWHERE

A SONG CAN GO ANYWHERE

AL VICENT

THIS THANKSGIVING DAY

THIS THANKSGIVING DAY

AL VICENT

CHRISTMAS TIME

CHRISTMAS TIME

AL VICENT

2

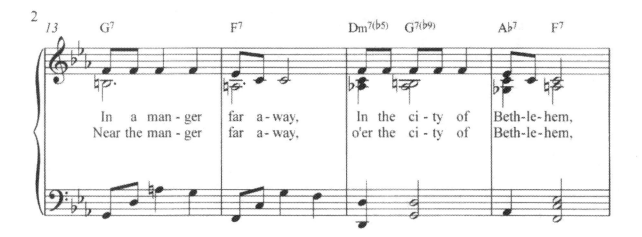

In a man - ger far a - way, In the ci - ty of Beth - le - hem,
Near the man - ger far a - way, o'er the ci - ty of Beth - le - hem,

God sent love to Earth that day, When Christ was born on Christ mas day.
Sang of love o'er the Earth that day, When Christ was born on Christ mas day.

Shep - herds came on Christ - mas day, To the man - ger far a - way,
Peace on Earth on Christ - mas day, from a man - ger far a - way,

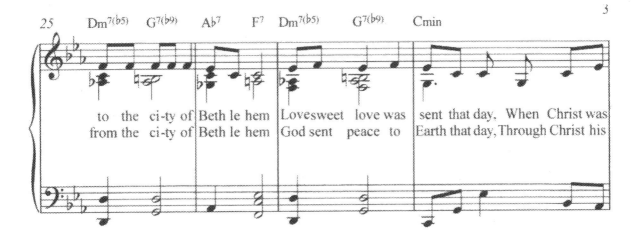

25 Dm⁷⁽ᵇ⁵⁾ G⁷⁽ᵇ⁹⁾ Ab⁷ F⁷ Dm⁷⁽ᵇ⁵⁾ G⁷⁽ᵇ⁹⁾ Cmin

to the ci-ty of Beth le hem | Love sweet love was | sent that day, When Christ was
from the ci-ty of Beth le hem | God sent peace to | Earth that day, Through Christ his

29 G⁷⁽ᵇ⁹⁾ F⁷ Cmin Eb F Eb

born on Christmas day. | Christmas time, | Christmas day that spe-cial | time when
child on Christmas day.

34 Ab⁷ Fmin/G Cmin Cmin F⁷

Christ was | born. | Christmas time is | here to stay. Our

4

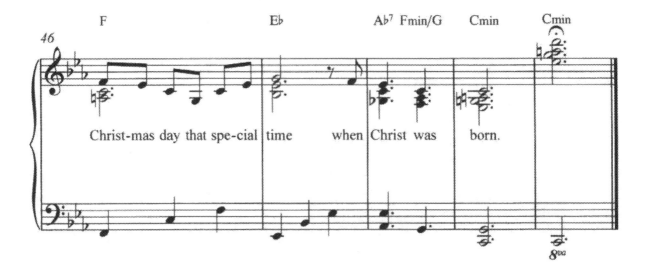

PRAY TO GOD

PRAY TO GOD

AL VICENT

Pray to God from where you are, He will
strength to all who pray, Gives them

hear you from a - far, Pray to God He hears your prayer, will be
strength in their own way, And they get spirit - ual strength that way, So pray to

with you and He'll care. Pray to God in your own way, Be sure you
God some-where to - day. God hears prayers of those who pray, and bless - es

pray to God each day, He hears all in His own way, So come and
them in His own way, Be sure you pray to God each day, He will

pray to Him to - day. Pray to God he lis-tens with you, To the
hear you when you pray.

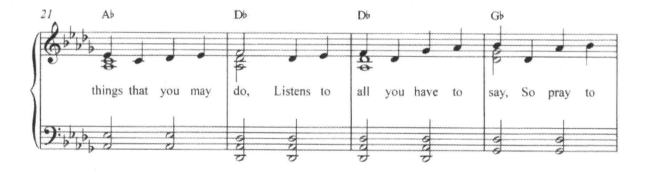

things that you may do, Listens to all you have to say, So pray to

1.
2.

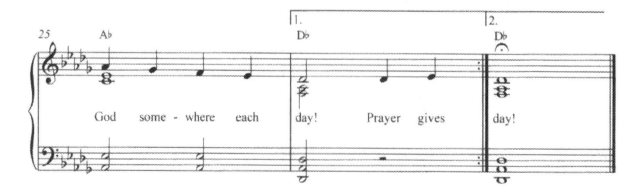

God some - where each day! Prayer gives day!

THE CRUCIFIXION

Arranged by Gianni Staiano

The following is a finalized version of the crucifixion. It is arranged by Gianni Staiano. It will shown in comparison to Al's originally written version and will demonstrate the way the music can change a small amount from the original to the finalized version.

THE CRUCIFIXION

Arranged by Gianni Staiano

AL VICENT

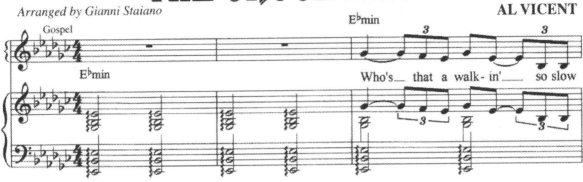

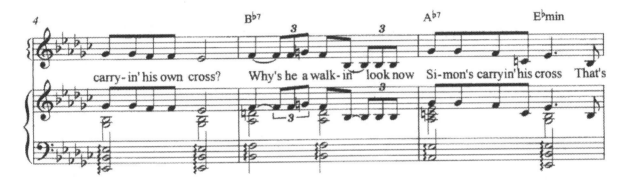

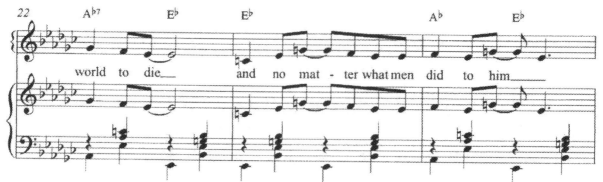

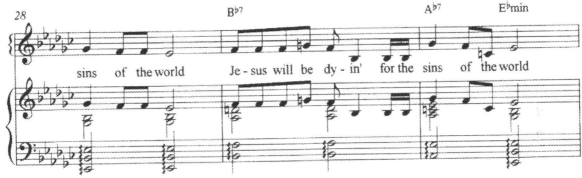

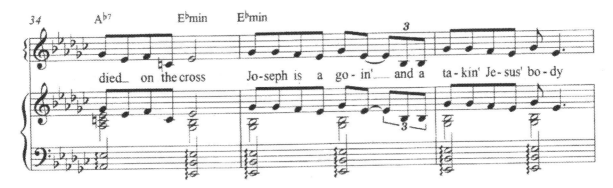

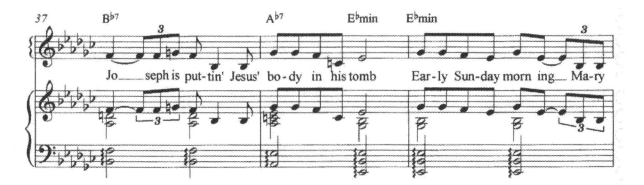

he'll   re - turn____   oh he'll come   back   a -   gain____

ORIGINAL VERSION

This version of the crucifixion is how it was originally written by Al. From this point on all the song will be the orginal versions by Al.

THE CRUCIFIXION

THE SPIRIT OF GOD

THE SPIRIT OF GOD

DRIV-IN' OUT HATE... THE SPIR-IT OF GOD... IT'S A MOV-IN' IN THE LAND. THE
FAM-I-LIES TO-GETH-ER... THE SPIR-IT OF GOD... IT'S A MOV-IN' IN THE LAND. THE

D.S. $\mathbf{\it ff}$ AL CODA

CODA

(5., 6.) SPIR-IT OF GOD... IT'S A MOV-IN' AND A RUMB-LIN'... THE SPIR-IT OF GOD... IT'S A

MOV-IN' IN THE LAND. THE SPIR-IT OF GOD... IS_ NEED-ED BY THE NAT-IONS. THE
THE SPIR-IT OF GOD GIVES LOV-IN' WORLD PEACE___ THE

SPIR-IT OF GOD... IT'S A MOV-IN' IN THE LAND. THE
SPIR-IT OF GOD... IT'S A MOV-IN' IN THE LAND. THE

D.S. $\mathbf{\it ff}$ AL FINE

110

LET YOUR LIGHT SHINE

LET YOUR LIGHT SHINE

Let your light shine

WORDS AND MUSIC BY
AL VICENT

MODERATO

BRIGHTEN YOUR DAY ___ I LIGHT A CANDLE TO DAY ___ I BRIGHTEN YOUR

DAY ___ I LIGHT A CANDLE TO DAY ___ BRIGHTEN THE DARK ___ LET YOUR LIGHT

SHINE ___ I BRIGHTEN YOUR DAY ___ LET YOUR LIGHT SHINE ___ SOME LOVE THE

DARK ___ GOD LOVES LIGHT ___ SOME LOVE THE DARK ___ OH ___ GOD LOVES

LIGHT ___ BRIGHTEN YOUR DAY ___ LET YOUR LIGHT SHINE ___ I BRIGHTEN THE

DAY ___ I LET YOUR LIGHT SHINE ___ WALK IN THE SPIR ___ IT ___ I GOD GIVES

LIGHT ___ I WALK IN THE SPIR ___ IT ___ I GOD GIVES LIGHT ___ BRIGHTEN THE DARK ___ I LET YOUR LIGHT

SHINE ___ I BRIGHTEN THE DAY ___ I LET YOUR LIGHT SHINE ___ MANS
fine

113

114

GO, TELL THE PEOPLE

GO, TELL THE PEOPLE
GO, TELL THE PEOPLE

WORDS AND MUSIC BY
AL VICENT

F   F7   Bb7

GO, TELL THE PEO-PLE A CHILD HAS BEEN BORN____.

C SUS   Db7   C7   F   Bb7   Bo

GO TELL THE PEO-PLE A CHILD HAS BEEN BORN....TELL ALL THE PEO-PLE A CHILD __

C+7   F   C SUS   Bb7

__ HAS BEEN BORN.. AND NOW, AND NOW, AND NOW IT'S CHRIST-MAS MORN __

F/C   Bb/C   Eb/C   F   F7   Bb7

GO, TELL THE PEO-PLE WHERE THE CHILD WAS BORN __

C SUS   Db7 C7   F   Bb7   Bo

TELL ALL THE PEO-PLE WHERE THE CHILD WAS BORN.. THE CHILD WAS BORN IN THE

C7   F   C SUS   Bb7   (3)

CI-TY OF BETH-LE-HEM, THE CHILD WAS BORN IN THE CI-TY OF BETH-LE-HEM __

F/C   Bb/C   Eb/C   C SUS   F   F7   Bb7

GO, TELL THE PEO-PLE WHO THE NEW CHILD IS ____.

C SUS   Db7 C7   F   Bb7   Bø7

GO, TELL THE PEO-PLE WHO THE NEW CHILD IS ____. THE CHILD IS THE SAV-IOR SENT FROM

117

C7 F C SUS Bb7 F
GOD A-BOVE __, THE CHILD IS THE SAV-IOR SENT FROM GOD A-BOVE __.
F F7 Bb7 Bø7 C SUS
GO, TELL THE PEO-PLE ALL THE AN-GELS ARE SING-ING __, TELL ALL THE PEO-PLE ALL THE
C7 F Bø7 Bbm6 Am7 Dm
AN-GELS ARE SING-ING __, GO, TELL THE PEO-PLE ALL THE SHEP-HERDS ARE COM-ING __,
Gm7 C7 Bb7 F7 C7 SUS 4
TELL ALL THE PEO-PLE THE SHEP-HERDS ARE COM-ING... TELL ALL __ THE PEO-
F
__ PLE __.

ROLL ON, CHARIOT

ROLL ON, CHARIOT

Roll On, Chariot

WORDS AND MUSIC BY
AL VICENT

LIVE ON __ I LIVE __ I TELL __ YOU..LIVE ON __ I LIVE __

__ I TELL __ YOU. SOON THE CHAR-I-OT WILL BE LAND-IN', BE

HEAD-ED FOR THE PROM-ISED LAND _____ TALK ON __ A

LIT-TLE BIT LONG __ ER __ TALK ON __ A __ LIT-TLE BIT LONG __ ER. SOON THE

CHAR-I-OT WILL BE LAND-IN', BE HEAD-ED FOR THE PROM-ISED LAND _____

CHORUS

ROLL ON, ROLL ... I ROLL ON CHAR-I-OT,

ROLL ON, ROLL ... I ROLL ON CHAR-I-OT, ROLL ON, ROLL

ROLL ON CHAR-I-OT CAR-RY ME TO THE PROM-ISED LAND ____ .

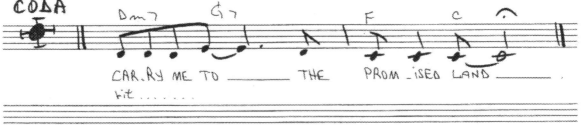

HOLD ON ___ A   LIT_TLE BIT LONG ___ ER ... HOLD ON ___ A
SING ON ___ A   LIT_TLE BIT LONG ___ ER ... SING ON ___ A

LIT_TLE BIT LONG ___ ER .. SOON THE CHAR_I_OT WILL BE LAND_IN'...BE
LIT_TLE BIT LONG ___ ER .. SOON THE CHAR_I_OT WILL BE LAND_IN...BE

HEAD_ED FOR THE PROM_ISED ___ LAND _____ .   SMILE ON ___ A
HEAD_ED FOR THE PROM_ISED ___ LAND _____ .   PRAY ON ___ A

LIT_TLE BIT LONG ___ ER.... SMILE ON ... A
LIT_TLE BIT LONG ___ ER.... PRAY ON ... A

LIT_TLE BIT LONG ___ ER .. SOON THE CHAR_I_OT WILL BE LAND_IN'...BE
LIT_TLE BIT LONG ___ ER .. SOON THE CHARI_OT WILL BE LAND_IN...BE

HEAD_ED FOR THE PROM_ISED ___ LAND _____ .   D.S. 'S' TWICE
HEAD_ED FOR THE PROM_ISED ___ LAND _____ .   TAKE CODA

CODA

CAR_RY ME TO ___ THE   PROM_ISED LAND _____
tit........

122

SOME SWEET DAY

SOME SWEET DAY
Some Sweet Day

WORDS AND MUSIC BY
AL VICENT

SLOW GOSPEL WALTZ WITH A BEAT

SOME SWEET DAY __ WHEN HE CALLS __ WE'LL BE
READY __ WHEN HE CALLS .. SOME SWEET DAY , SOME SWEET DAY __ WHEN HE
CALLS __ ..SOME SWEET DAY __ ..WE'LL MEET ON THE OTH-ER SIDE WITH SWEET
JE-SUS , THERE WE'LL A BIDE ...SOME SWEET DAY __ ..SOME SWEET DAY __ WHEN HE
CALLS __ SOME SWEET DAY __ WE'LL MEET ON THE OTH-ER
SIDE __ WITH THE SPIR_IT WE WILL A_ BIDE ..SOME SWEET DAY , SOME SWEET
DAY __ WHEN HE CALLS __ SOME SWEET DAY .. IN THE DARK __ ON SOME
NIGHT __ YOU JUST MIGHT SEE HIS LIGHT ..SOME SWEET DAY , SOME SWEET

DAY ____ WHEN HE CALLS ... SOME SWEET DAY . PRAY ON . PRAY AND BE

REA_DY .. JE_SUS WILL COME.. YOU BE REA_DY ... SOME SWEET

DAY ... SOME SWEET DAY ____ WHEN HE CALLS ____ SOME SWEET DAY, WE'LL

D.S. AL
Fine

LOVE

WAITIN'
(FOR SALINAS TRAIN)

I'm waitin' for
The Train
I'm waintin' for
The Train
I'm waitin' for
The Train to Salinas

Oh where– oh where
Oh where– oh where
Oh where in the world
Is Salinas

It's way out West
Where the Broccoli grows

It's way out west
Where there's Cowboys too

It's way out west
That's the place for you

Way out West
In Salinas

What will you do
When you get out there

What will you do in Salinas

I'll pretend I'm a cowboy
When I get out there

Ride and old grey horse
That's and an old grey mare

That's what I'll do
I'll do, I'll do
That's what I'll do
When I get to Salinas.

Waitin'

Albert Vicent

Printed in the United States
by Baker & Taylor Publisher Services